ENERGY

INTRODUCTION TO PHYSICS

ENERGY

EDITED BY ANDREA R. FIELD

Britannica
Educational Publishing
IN ASSOCIATION WITH
ROSEN
EDUCATIONAL SERVICES

Published in 2012 by Britannica Educational Publishing
(a trademark of Encyclopædia Britannica, Inc.)
in association with Rosen Educational Services, LLC
29 East 21st Street, New York, NY 10010.

Distributed exclusively by Rosen Educational Services.
For a listing of additional Britannica Educational Publishing titles, call toll free (800) 237-9932.

First Edition

Britannica Educational Publishing
Michael I. Levy: Executive Editor, Encyclopædia Britannica
J.E. Luebering: Director, Core Reference Group, Encyclopædia Britannica
Adam Augustyn: Assistant Manager, Encyclopædia Britannica

Anthony L. Green: Editor, Compton's by Britannica
Michael Anderson: Senior Editor, Compton's by Britannica
Andrea R. Field: Senior Editor, Compton's by Britannica
Sherman Hollar: Associate Editor, Compton's by Britannica

Marilyn L. Barton: Senior Coordinator, Production Control
Steven Bosco: Director, Editorial Technologies
Lisa S. Braucher: Senior Producer and Data Editor
Yvette Charboneau: Senior Copy Editor
Kathy Nakamura: Manager, Media Acquisition

Rosen Educational Services
Jeanne Nagle: Senior Editor
Nelson Sá: Art Director
Cindy Reiman: Photography Manager
Karen Huang: Photo Researcher
Brian Garvey: Designer, Cover Design
Introduction by Jeanne Nagle

Library of Congress Cataloging-in-Publication Data

Energy/edited by Andrea R. Field.—1st ed.
    p. cm.—(Introduction to physics)
Includes bibliographical references and index.
ISBN 978-1-61530-673-2 (library binding)
1. Force and energy—Study and teaching (Middle school) I. Field, Andrea R.
QC73.6.E536 2012
531'.6—dc23

2011021493

Manufactured in the United States of America

On the cover, page 3: A gymnast in repose illustrates potential energy, while the ribbon she twirls
demonstrates kinetic energy. *Shutterstock.com*

Pages 6-7: A catapult releases its payload, illustrating how potential energy—created when the catapult is
pulled back and readied—changes to kinetic energy. *Steve Bronstein/The Image Bank/Getty Images*

Cover (equation) *Shutterstock.com*; pp. 10, 21, 34, 48, 58 *iStockphoto/Thinkstock*; remaining interior background images *Shutterstock.com*

CONTENTS

E very day, children around the world are encouraged by their parents to go outside and play, to "burn off some energy." But in the world of physics, energy is described in terms of work, not play. In physics, energy equals the ability to do work.

Truth be told, work means something a bit different to physicists than it does to the average person. In their vocabulary, work is not just doing tasks and keeping busy. For work to be involved, there has to be some kind of force that causes an object to move. Mathematically, if the object is moved in the same direction as the force, this is described as $W = Fs$—work equals force times the distance (represented by s) moved. In other words, work is measured by how strong the force is and how far the object moves. The more work done on an object, the more energy it has.

Making this concept even more interesting is the fact that energy is not just one thing. There are different types of energy. The earlier idea of children playing comes in handy when describing the forms of energy. For instance, there is kinetic energy, which is the energy associated with motion. Running from third base to home plate while playing baseball is a good example of kinetic energy. So are riding a bike and swimming in a pool.

Then there is potential energy. This occurs when an object is positioned in such a way that its energy will increase once it is "forced" into motion. In other words, the object has energy because of its potential for movement. On the playground, a swing set provides an excellent example of potential energy. Pushing a swing puts it in motion, creating kinetic energy. But at the height of its motion—when in a position to be pulled in a downward arc by gravity—the swing has potential energy. Likewise, a child sitting at the top of a slide has potential energy before he or she glides down its surface to the ground.

Kinetic and potential energy are the two most basic forms of energy, but there are others. Chemical energy is present whenever atoms are combined to form molecules, which make up the cells of every living thing. It is the chemical energy stored in a child's muscles that enable him or her to push a swing or run around a baseball diamond. As a bat or tennis racket strikes a ball, it gives off heat energy. Radiant energy is released by the Sun that shines, making outdoor play possible, while electrical energy is contained in bolts of lightning during a thunderstorm that sends everyone scurrying inside.

Another interesting fact about energy is that it has the ability to change from one form to another. As mentioned before, a child sitting on top of a slide has potential energy. That potential energy turns to kinetic energy as soon as he or she begins sliding down. Within an energy system—a group of objects that transfer energy back and forth among themselves—energy may move from one part to another, but the total amount of energy in the system does not change.

Studying physics certainly is not child's play, meaning it is not simple or unimportant. But with a little imagination, the idea of children playing can help make the concept of energy come alive.

CHAPTER 1

ENERGY BASICS

A rock falling off a cliff is different from the same rock lying on the ground below. A rubber band pulled taut is different from the same rubber band left slack. A glowing lightbulb is different from the same bulb when the electricity is switched off. It is the same rock, the same rubber band, the same lightbulb. The difference is one of energy.

Energy is one of the most basic ideas of science. All activity in the universe can be explained in terms of energy and matter. But the definition of energy is not at all simple, since energy occurs in many different forms, and it is not always easy to tell how these forms are related to one another and what they have in common. One of the best-known definitions of energy is the classical definition used in physics: Energy is the ability to do work.

The many forms of energy include kinetic, potential, chemical, nuclear, electrical, light, heat, and sound energy. All these types of energy can do work.

Energy is the difference between the glowing bulb in the center and the dark ones that surround it. Shutterstock.com

ENERGY SYSTEMS

Energy is readily transferred from object to object, especially in the form of heat. For this reason, it is often necessary to study an entire group of objects that may be transferring energy back and forth among themselves. Such a group is called a system. The energy of a system is the ability of the entire system

DEFINING WORK

Physicists define work in a way that does not always agree with the average person's idea of work. In physics, work is done when a force applied to an object moves it some distance in the direction of the force. Mathematically, $W = Fs$, where W is the work done, F is the force applied, and s is the distance moved. If either F or s is equal to zero, W is also equal to zero, so no work is done.

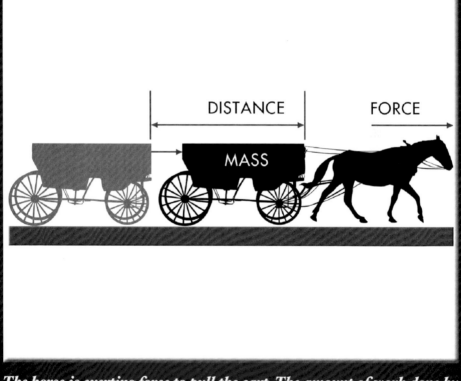

The horse is exerting force to pull the cart. The amount of work done by the horse is equal to the force exerted times the distance the cart is pulled. Copyright Encyclopædia Britannica; rendering for this edition by Rosen Educational Services

Holding weights steady at shoulder level might qualify as a workout, but it does not meet the physics definition of work. Jupiterimages/ Comstock/Thinkstock

If a person walks up a flight of stairs, he may regard it as work—he exerts effort to move his body to a higher level. In this instance, he also does work according to the definition accepted by physicists because he exerts a force to lift himself over a distance — the distance from the bottom to the top of the stairs.

However, if a person stands without moving with a 100-pound (45-kilogram) weight in her outstretched arms, she is not doing any work as physicists define work. She is exerting a force that keeps the weight from falling to the floor, but the position of the weight remains unchanged. It is not moved any distance by the force. The person is, of course, exerting considerable muscular effort to avoid dropping the weight, and the average person would say that she is working very hard indeed. But she is not doing any work according to the definition accepted in physics.

to do work. If the parts of a system do work on one another but do not change anything outside the system, then the total amount of energy in the system stays the same. However, the amount of energy in one part of the system may decrease and the amount of energy of another part may increase.

Consider a system consisting of a rainforest with many trees, a vine hanging from the central tree, the ground supporting the trees, and a monkey standing beneath the tree from which the vine is hanging. The monkey, holding the free end of the vine, climbs up the central tree. It then moves several treetops away, maintaining the same altitude. Finally, the monkey grasps the vine that is still tied to the central tree and swings down, past the central tree, and up again until it lands in a third tree. An observer watching the monkey swinging from one tree to the other will conclude that the system possesses energy and can do work.

The necessary elements in this system are the monkey, the trees, Earth, and the vine. The monkey provides the initial energy by climbing the trees, while the trees support the monkey against the force of gravity, which pulls downward. Earth's gravitational attraction is the force that draws the monkey downward once it begins to swing on the vine. The vine supports the monkey so that it remains free to swing upward against the force of gravity and into another tree. When all these elements occur together, the system is capable of doing work; it has energy.

KINETIC AND POTENTIAL ENERGY

As the monkey swings on the vine, it is acting like a pendulum. Like any pendulum, it is exhibiting the difference between two kinds of energy—kinetic energy and potential energy.

Kinetic energy is the energy of motion. While the monkey is swinging from one tree to the other, it has kinetic energy. So, too, does a speeding bus, a falling raindrop, and a spinning top. Any moving object has this type of energy.

Potential energy is the energy an object or system has because of the position of its parts. It is often thought of as "stored" energy (though it is important to remember that energy is not a substance). For example, a stretched spring has potential energy. Force has been applied to stretch the spring, creating stored energy. The more the spring is stretched from its normal position, the greater its capacity to do work when released. Likewise, a steel ball has more potential

As this orangutan swings from treetops to vines, it becomes an intricate part of this jungle energy system. Hemera/Thinkstock

energy raised above the ground than it has after falling to Earth. In the raised position, it is capable of doing more work because of the pull of gravity.

The monkey also has potential energy as it stands in the treetop. The monkey is not moving, so it has no kinetic energy. But the system has energy because of the monkey's location above the ground. The work done to lift the monkey against the force of gravity has created potential energy.

The potential energy is released when the monkey jumps off the tree. Gravity pulls it downward, and it swings faster and faster until, as it sweeps by the ground, it is traveling very fast. In place of the lost potential energy, the system has gained more and more kinetic energy from the speed of the monkey's motion. When the

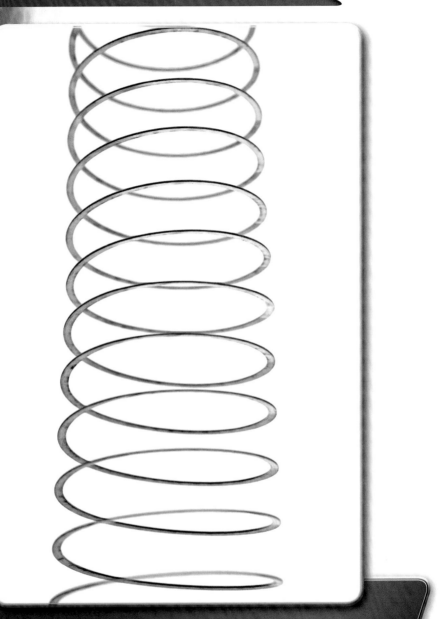

A spring toy, stretched from end to end. Stretching changes the form and position of the spring, creating potential or "stored" energy. Shutterstock.com

monkey lands in the next tree, the system again has potential energy but no kinetic energy.

This example demonstrates a basic property of energy—one form of energy can be changed into another. In this case, potential energy was converted to kinetic energy, which was then changed back into potential energy.

A hammer driving a nail into a board illustrates the concept of mechanical energy. Shutterstock.com

MECHANICAL ENERGY

The term "mechanical energy" can be applied to systems in which all the significant components (such as the monkey, trees, Earth, and vine) are visible to the naked eye. Mechanical energy is equal to kinetic energy plus potential energy. It is thus all the energy an object has because of its motion and its position. Machines—from simple tools such as wedges, levers, and pulleys, to complex devices such as automobiles—use mechanical energy to do work.

A hammer uses mechanical energy to drive a nail into a board. When raised above the nail, the hammer has potential energy from the work done in lifting it. When the hammer is moved toward the nail, the potential energy becomes kinetic energy, which can do the work of driving the nail. Contact between the hammer and the nail transfers energy to the nail and then to the board.

CHAPTER 2

CHEMICAL AND NUCLEAR ENERGY

E ach of the various forms of energy can be described as either of the two basic energy forms: potential or kinetic. Chemical and nuclear energy both can be considered forms of microscopic potential ("stored") energy. Chemical energy is stored in the bonds of chemical compounds and may be released during a chemical reaction, when the compounds are changed. Nuclear energy is stored within the cores of the tiny units of matter known as atoms. Large amounts of energy are released during nuclear reactions, when changes occur in the core of the atom.

CHEMICAL ENERGY

When several chemicals are mixed together to form gunpowder or dynamite, a violent explosion can occur if care is not taken to prevent this. An explosion can do work against the force of gravity, for example, by

Sticks of dynamite are formed when nitroglycerin is mixed with diatomaceous earth and stuffed into a casing with a fuse attached. Also created by this mixture is chemical energy. Shutterstock.com

throwing pieces of material into the air. A mixture of chemicals that can do work is said to have chemical energy. But not all chemical systems that can do work are as dramatically energetic as gunpowder or dynamite.

To understand chemical energy, it is necessary to study what happens during a chemical reaction. An atom can bond to other atoms to form a group called a molecule. Atoms and molecules are the basic building blocks of all matter. Chemical energy is what holds the atoms in a molecule together.

For example, one kind of atom is the oxygen atom (O). An oxygen atom and two hydrogen atoms (H_2) combine to form a water molecule (H_2O). One kind of sand molecule, silicon dioxide (SiO_2), contains one atom of silicon (Si) and two atoms of oxygen.

Molecules are formed in chemical reactions. Some molecules give off a great deal of energy when they are formed. Such molecules are very stable because all that energy must be put back into them before they break apart. Other molecules release very little energy when they are formed. Such molecules are very unstable. They react easily to form more stable molecules. During these reactions, much energy is given off. Nitroglycerin—a dense, oily liquid—changes readily to water, carbon dioxide, nitrogen, and oxygen. This reaction is explosive because it occurs very rapidly and because the suddenly formed gases take up much more room than did the liquid nitroglycerin. Other chemical reactions can produce energy but not be explosive. They may occur more slowly, and the resulting

As a sheep grazes on hillside grass, it ingests chemical energy that the grass created via photosynthesis. Shutterstock.com

molecules may take up the same amount of room as the original molecules.

Food energy is a form of chemical energy. Plants absorb energy from sunlight and store it in energy-rich chemicals, such as glucose. This process is called photosynthesis. Animals that eat plants use the chemicals created by photosynthesis to maintain life processes. Other animals may eat plant-eating animals to gain the energy-rich chemicals that the plant-eaters formed from the chemicals of plants. Since food energy is what keeps living things moving, it is clearly able to do work.

NUCLEAR ENERGY

Yet another kind of energy is stored in the small, dense centers of atoms. The core of an atom is known as its nucleus (plural: nuclei). Nuclear energy is the energy that holds the nucleus together. This energy is released when the nucleus is rearranged. The nucleus contains two kinds of particles called protons and neutrons. Some nuclei spontaneously rearrange, losing some particles and emitting energy. This process is called radioactivity. For example, a nucleus of the element radium can spontaneously eject a cluster

FOSSIL FUELS

Humans transform the many kinds of energy in nature to produce a variety of fuels and other power sources. Energy-conversion systems power automobiles and airplanes, for example, and provide buildings with heating and

A pump pulling oil from deep underground. Shutterstock.com

electric power. Some of these conversion systems are quite complex, requiring multiple steps in which energy undergoes a whole series of transformations through various forms. The most common sources of power in the industrial world—including coal, petroleum (oil), and natural gas—are fossil fuels. The use of these fuels releases chemical energy that was produced by living things long ago through photosynthesis. Fossil fuels are found in Earth's crust. They are the end product of the remains of plants, algae, bacteria, and other organisms buried millions of years ago. Over time, chemical and geological processes slowly transformed the remains into fuels.

All fossil fuels contain carbon. To provide power, they are burned in air. The fuels combine with the oxygen from the air in a chemical reaction, transforming chemical energy into heat energy. This energy may be used directly, such as in home furnaces. In other cases, the heat energy is converted to mechanical energy. In a typical automobile engine, the combustion (burning) of gasoline creates hot gases. These hot gases expand rapidly, generating a force that is used to move pistons. The resulting mechanical energy is used to propel the car.

In electric power plants that use fossil fuels, an additional energy conversion is required. First, the coal, oil, or natural gas is burned to produce steam. The steam expands in a turbine, a device that converts the heat energy to mechanical energy. The turbine is connected to a generator. As the turbine spins, it turns a revolving part in the generator. Finally, the mechanical energy is converted to electrical energy in the generator.

of two neutrons and two protons (called an alpha particle) and a gamma ray (a type of electromagnetic radiation). These carry away

The U.S.S. Montpelier *nuclear submarine docks at Souda Harbor in Greece. Long-lasting energy from a nuclear reactor inside the vessel allows the sub greater underwater capability and virtually unlimited range.* **U.S. Navy photo by Mr. Paul Farley**

energy from the nucleus, which changes into a smaller, more stable form.

Nuclear reactions fuel the Sun and other stars. People use nuclear energy in nuclear power plants that produce electricity and in nuclear weapons. Nuclear energy also powers some vehicles, such as nuclear submarines. Two techniques allow people to release nuclear energy through nuclear reactions. The first, called fission, involves splitting a nucleus into two fragments. The second involves combining two nuclei to form one nucleus. This technique is called fusion. Both techniques have been used to make bombs, but only fission has been used successfully in power plants and vehicles.

FISSION

Fission makes use of elements with very heavy atoms, such as uranium. A large amount of energy is required to hold together the nucleus of such a heavy atom. In fact, more energy is required to hold together the uranium nucleus than to hold together two nuclei that are half the size of a uranium nucleus.

In atomic bombs and fission reactors at nuclear power plants, uranium atoms are bombarded with particles, such as free neutrons. When a neutron hits a nucleus, the nucleus splits into two smaller nuclei, releasing a great deal of energy. In the reaction, some of the neutrons of the uranium nucleus fly off and hit other nuclei. These collisions in turn cause the other nuclei to split in two and release more energy and more neutrons. The process can continue explosively, as it does in an atomic bomb. In nuclear reactors, the fission must be controlled. Typically, metal rods are inserted to capture some of the neutrons and slow down the reaction.

FUSION

The second kind of nuclear reaction is harder to produce and control. It makes use of very small nuclei, such as those of hydrogen. If two hydrogen nuclei can be combined to form one heavier nucleus, a large amount of energy is released. This type of reaction occurs in the Sun. By a

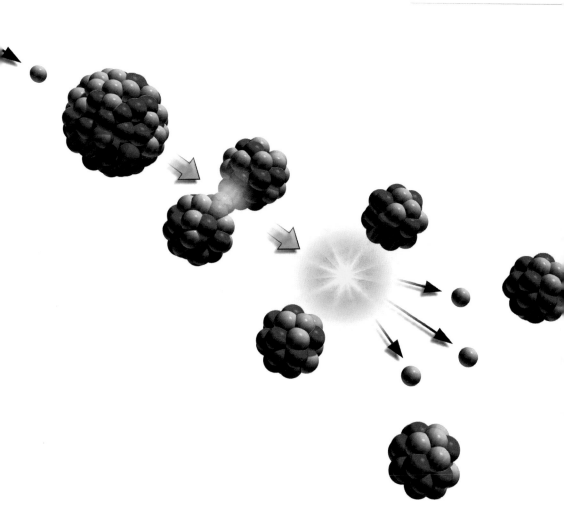

Graphic illustration of a nuclear fission chain reaction.
Shutterstock.com

NUCLEAR POWER

About one-sixth of the world's electric power plants use nuclear energy to make electricity. First, nuclear energy is converted to heat energy in a fission reaction. Heat is transferred to a coolant, which also helps to control the reaction. The coolant then transfers some of the heat to water to produce steam. As in power plants that use fossil fuels, the steam expands in a turbine, making the turbine spin. Heat energy is thus converted to mechanical energy. The spinning turbine turns a part in a connected generator, and the generator converts the mechanical energy to electrical energy. Most nuclear power plants use enriched uranium as the fuel and ordinary water as the coolant.

somewhat complicated series of reactions, four hydrogen nuclei join together to form a new helium nucleus, giving off a great deal of energy in the process. This joining of nuclei is the source of all the energy emitted by the Sun.

Temperatures in this kind of reaction must be very high (in the millions of degrees) before the nuclei have enough energy to collide with the force needed for them to join together. The reaction is called a thermonuclear fusion reaction. "Thermonuclear" refers to the heat required for the nuclei to

The experimental detonation of an atomic bomb on Enewetak atoll in 1952. United States Department of Energy

react, and "fusion" means that in the reaction nuclei join together.

A thermonuclear fusion reaction occurs when a hydrogen bomb explodes. Scientists are trying to develop a way of releasing energy by fusion reactions under controlled conditions, in order to produce electrical power. Fusion reactions release far more energy than fission reactions do.

CHAPTER 3

ELECTRICAL, RADIANT, AND HEAT ENERGY

Among the other forms of energy are electrical, radiant, and heat energy. The energy of a lightning bolt is an example of electrical energy. People make use of this kind of energy with batteries, electrical generators, and other devices that produce electricity. Radiant energy is transmitted by light, X-rays, radio waves, and some other types of radiation emitted in waves. Heat energy, or thermal energy, is the internal energy an object or system has because of its temperature.

ELECTRICAL ENERGY

The use of electrical energy is very important in the modern industrial world. Electric currents turn motors and drive machinery. Electric currents provide the energy of labor-saving appliances such as power tools, vacuum cleaners, and dishwashers. Clearly, the currents can do work and thus possess energy.

Bolts of lightning flashing over a city skyline are a dramatic representation of electrical energy. Shutterstock.com

An electric current is a stream of moving particles or atoms that carry an electrical charge. Electrical energy is linked with the basic structure of the atom. The nucleus at the center of the atom is heavy and positively charged. One or more light, negatively charged particles called electrons circulate around the nucleus. The positively charged nucleus and the negatively charged electrons attract one another. This attraction keeps most of the electrons circulating near the nucleus. But sometimes a neighboring nucleus will also attract the electrons of the first atom. This is how a chemical bond is formed. So, in a way, all chemical energy is a special, microscopic kind of electrical energy.

Metals are made up of atoms that contain many electrons. Because of the peculiar structure of metal atoms, the atomic nuclei are not strong enough to hold on to all their electrons. Some of the electrons more or less float from nucleus to nucleus. These free electrons can take part in an electric current.

Batteries have both a positive (+) and a negative (-) terminal. Connecting the two allows for the free flow of electrons, which creates an electrical charge. Shutterstock.com

Work must be done to separate negative and positive charges if one is to produce a surplus of electrons in one place and of nuclei that are missing one or more electrons in another place. When this situation occurs, as in a battery, energy is stored. One end of a metal wire may be connected to the place where excess electrons are collected (the negative terminal on a battery). The other end of the wire is connected to the place where excess electron-deficient nuclei are collected (the positive terminal on a battery). The electrons in the wire flow to join the nuclei. Electrons farther down the wire flow after the first electrons, and the electrons from the battery move into the wire. The total electron flow from the negative terminal of the battery through the wire and into the positive terminal is an electric current. Since a force is applied that makes the electrons move a certain distance down the wire, work is done.

Magnetic energy is closely related to electrical energy. Magnetic fields are set up whenever electric charges move.

RADIANT ENERGY

Light is one type of electromagnetic radiation. Some other kinds of radiation include

X-rays, radio waves, and microwaves. Radiant energy is the energy transmitted by electromagnetic radiation. This kind of energy travels in waves. It can travel through empty space, air, or even solid substances. Radiant energy is caused by accelerated electric charges or by electric or magnetic fields that increase or decrease with time.

The motion of these charges and fields disturbs space. The disturbance causes a wave to travel away from the site of the original electrical or magnetic motion. The wave consists of growing and collapsing electric and magnetic fields that are oriented at right angles to one another.

Light is the only form of electromagnetic radiation that is visible to the naked eye. Some forms of electromagnetic radiation have longer wavelengths than light. They include radio waves, microwaves, and infrared rays. Gamma rays, X-rays, and ultraviolet radiation have shorter wavelengths than light.

Although electromagnetic radiation can be described as traveling in continuous waves, it can also be described as consisting of separate particles. These particles are tiny packets of energy called photons. Light

The Very Large Array 27-antenna radio telescope near Socorro, N.M., is used to detect radio frequency radiation—radiant energy— emitted by sources in outer space. **Space Frontiers/Archive Photos/Getty Images**

and other forms of electromagnetic radiation actually have some properties of waves and some properties of particles.

The amount of energy in a photon varies with the type of radiation. Forms of electromagnetic radiation with longer wavelengths have photons with lower energy, while forms with shorter wavelengths have photons with higher energy. Radio waves thus have low-energy photons, while gamma rays have high-energy photons.

All of the forms of radiant energy are able to do work. People use a variety of devices to capture and transform this energy. These devices generally change radiant energy to electrical energy, as in radios, televisions, cell phones, and solar cells, for example.

HEAT ENERGY

Molecules are always in motion. Heat energy, or thermal energy, is the energy something has because of the motion of its individual molecules. In other words, heat energy is the kinetic energy of the molecules. However, the molecules do not move

RENEWABLE ENERGY SOURCES

The supply of fossil fuels is limited. For this reason, they are called a nonrenewable energy source. Unfortunately, modern civilization has been using up in a few centuries the fossil fuels created over millions of years. In addition, the use of fossil fuels causes air pollution, acid rain, and global warming.

On the other hand, the energy sources known as renewable can be replenished easily and within a short time period. Sunshine and wind, for example, are extremely abundant. Other sources of renewable energy include rivers, tides, and hot springs. In addition to being renewable, these energy sources emit virtually no pollutants.

Solar collectors capture the radiant energy in sunlight and convert it to heat energy. This energy can be used to heat water and buildings, or can be further converted to mechanical and finally electrical energy. In solar plants, as in other electric power plants, steam is used to power a turbine, which drives an electrical generator.

Solar cells convert the radiant energy from sunlight directly to electrical energy. Light striking the cells knocks electrons out of their atoms to produce an electric voltage. However, the solar cells presently in use are not very efficient. They are used mainly in low-power applications, such as calculators, or in remote areas.

Wind, water (river), and tidal power all make use of mechanical energy. This energy is converted to electrical energy to produce electricity. The movement of the wind or the water in a river or ocean is used to turn a turbine connected to an electrical generator. Water power is also known as hydroelectric power.

Geothermal electricity is obtained by using heat from Earth's interior, usually at hot springs or geysers. Heat energy, which is also called thermal energy, is converted to mechanical and then electrical energy: steam is used to power a turbine, which in turn powers a generator.

together in one particular direction; they move randomly in all different directions. All matter has heat energy, since the molecules that make up matter are always moving.

Like all other forms of energy, heat energy can do work. When heat is applied to a liquid, the liquid may eventually boil, changing to a gas that takes up more space than does the liquid. The gas from a boiling liquid can exert great force. It drives the turbines that generate the electricity of large cities.

Most of the time that energy is used to do work, part of the energy is wasted as heat. For example, when a hammer is used to pound a nail into a board, much of the energy of the hammer goes to heating

44

Turbines of a Canadian nuclear power plant. Steam produced by the plant's nuclear reactors is delivered to turbines through big silver pipes (background), causing the turbines to turn and convert heat to mechanical energy. **Bloomberg via Getty Images**

up the nail, the head of the hammer, and the parts of the board that touch the nail. Only a small part of the total energy actually moves the nail into the board.

Excess heat energy from a car's engine—that which is not changed to mechanical energy to make the car run—is expelled through the tailpipe as exhaust fumes. Shutterstock.com

The same is true of an automobile engine. Such engines would be much more efficient if all of the chemical energy generated by the explosion of gasoline and air was ultimately changed to the mechanical energy that moves the pistons. The chemical energy is first converted to heat energy, some of which is then converted to mechanical energy. Much of the heat energy, however, is not transformed and is of no help in running the car.

CHAPTER 4

THE CHANGING FORMS OF ENERGY

O ne of the most useful properties of energy is that it can be changed from one form to another. These changes are happening all the time. Most machines have as their purpose the conversion of energy from one form to another.

Furthermore, even in ordinary activities, energy changes form. A person opening a door uses chemical energy stored in muscle tissues. This energy is converted to the mechanical energy of the moving muscle (as well as to heat energy). The muscle applies a force—a push—to the door and the door swings open. If the door bangs against a wall, some of its mechanical energy is changed to sound energy.

THE CONSERVATION OF ENERGY

Over centuries of scientific observation, scientists have noticed that energy seems to act in certain uniform ways. A regularity exists in its behavior to which no exceptions have been observed. This regularity

Wind turbines are machines that work by converting one kind of energy into another. The wind turns the turbine's blades, producing mechanical energy. An attached generator then changes this mechanical energy to electrical energy. **Bloomberg via Getty Image**

has been expressed in the law of the conservation of energy. The law asserts that the total energy of an isolated system does not change. (An isolated system does not have any interaction with what surrounds it. An insulated glass container, such as a Thermos, is considered an isolated system; it doesn't let cool air in or heat out.) In other words, the energy can be redistributed or can change from one form to another, but the total energy remains the same. When a system is not isolated, however, outside forces are able to act on it. In such instances, any change in the energy of the system must exactly equal the work done on it by the outside forces.

The law of the conservation of energy is remarkable because it states that a certain numerical quantity is unchanged throughout all processes. It does not say why or how this happens. It just says that while the forms of energy are constantly changing, energy itself can neither appear out of nowhere nor vanish into nowhere. Despite the great diversity of energy forms, scientists were able to establish that an amount of one kind of energy had exact equivalents in the other kinds of energy.

In addition, 20th-century scientists discovered that energy can be converted to matter as mass, and that mass can be converted to energy. Energy can thus be considered equivalent to mass.

The momentum of a ball swung from one end of a Newton's cradle will cause the last ball at the other end to swing, though the balls in between will remain motionless. Potential energy is changed to kinetic energy and back again, but the total amount of energy remains the same. Shutterstock.com

What makes the law of the conservation of energy so remarkable is that most of the other quantities that physicists measure are not necessarily conserved. Velocities, accelerations, temperatures, and chemical units, such as atoms and molecules, are not always conserved. However, the amount of matter in a system, like the amount of energy, is also conserved unless some of the matter is changed to energy, or some of the energy is changed to matter. To take account of such changes, the law of the conservation of energy is combined with the law of the conservation of mass to form an expanded law of the conservation of mass-energy.

MECHANICAL SYSTEMS AND FRICTION

The simplest examples of the conservation of energy are provided by systems in which only mechanical forces are acting. A swinging pendulum continually interchanges kinetic and potential energy. At the top of the swing, the velocity is zero and the energy is purely potential. At the bottom of the swing, the energy is purely kinetic. At positions in between, the energy is partly

MASS AND ENERGY

For hundreds of years, scientists thought that matter and energy were completely different from each other. But early in the 20th century, Albert Einstein concluded that matter and energy were closely related. He realized that mass could change to energy and energy could change to mass. Einstein described the relationship between mass and energy in the famous equation $E = mc^2$. In this equation, E stands for energy, m for mass, and c for the speed of light (which is a constant). The change in mass that is given by this equation is $m = E/c^2$. Since c^2 is a very large quantity, E must be very large indeed for m to be observable. This relationship has been experimentally confirmed.

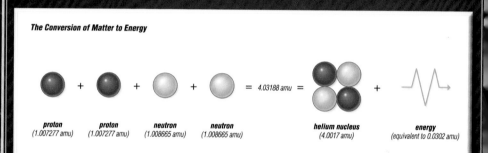

The Conversion of Matter to Energy

proton (1.007277 amu) + proton (1.007277 amu) + neutron (1.008665 amu) + neutron (1.008665 amu) = 4.03188 amu = helium nucleus (4.0017 amu) + energy (equivalent to 0.0302 amu)

When two protons and two neutrons are joined in a helium nucleus, their mass (expressed in atomic mass units, or amu) is slightly smaller. The difference has been converted into energy. The helium nucleus is very stable. **Encyclopædia Britannica, Inc.**

Chemical and nuclear reactions both involve a change in energy linked with a change in mass. Both may involve a reaction in which two entities form two new entities. In a chemical reaction, the entities are atoms or molecules. In a nuclear reaction, they are nuclei. In both cases, the reaction may end up with a loss of mass. This loss is converted to energy, usually in the form of the kinetic energy of the two new entities.

In a nuclear reaction, the loss in mass is about a million times larger than the loss in chemical reactions and is readily observable. Nuclear physicists routinely take account of the conversion of mass to energy in their study of nuclear reactions. However, the only difference between the loss of mass in chemical and nuclear reactions is a difference of magnitude. The source of both chemical and nuclear reactions is the same: the transformation of a certain amount of mass into energy.

potential and partly kinetic. However, the sum of the kinetic and the potential energy—the mechanical energy—is constant throughout.

Actually, very few examples exist of purely mechanical systems. A pendulum does not keep on swinging forever. After a while the swings get smaller, and eventually they stop. This happens because the mechanical energy of the pendulum is changed to heat energy by a force called friction, which is a force that resists the sliding or rolling of one object over another. This force changes mechanical energy to heat energy whenever two pieces of matter move up against one another, such as when a person rubs his or her hands together to warm them.

The pendulum of a metronome in action. Although the amounts of kinetic and potential energy are continually changing as the pendulum moves, the mechanical energy (the sum of the kinetic and potential energy) remains constant. Shutterstock.com

The motion of the pendulum is slowed by the friction it experiences when it moves through the air and rubs against the hook that holds it up. The energy of the pendulum is transferred to the molecules of the air through which it moves and to the molecules

Friction converts the mechanical energy from quickly and suddenly rotating car tires to heat energy. The heat breaks the bonds of rubber in the tires and leaves skid marks on the road.
Shutterstock.com

of the hook. These molecules move faster, and the temperature of the air and the hook rises. Mechanical energy has been changed to heat energy.

Friction plays a role in most mechanical situations. It may change some or all of the mechanical energy of the system to heat energy. For example, if a nail is driven into a wall, the work done by the hammer goes into energy of deformation (the nail changes the form of the wall as it moves through it) and into a large amount of heat. The nail and the head of the hammer grow hot.

CHAPTER 5

THE LAWS OF THERMODYNAMICS

I n the early 19th century, the Industrial Revolution was well underway. The many newly invented machines of the time were powered by the burning of fuel. These machines provided scientists with a great deal of information about how heat energy could be converted to other types of energy, how other types of energy could be converted to heat energy, and how heat energy could do work. Some of these observations were condensed into the laws of thermodynamics, which is the branch of physics that studies relationships between heat energy, other forms of energy, and work.

THE FIRST LAW

The first law of thermodynamics is a mathematical statement of the conservation of energy. This law states that the amount of

James Joule established that the various forms of energy are basically the same and can be changed, one into another—thereby forming the basis of the first law of thermodynamics. SSPL via Getty Images

heat added to a system exactly equals any change in energy of the system plus all the work done by the system. The practical importance of the first law of thermodynamics is that it shows that the addition of heat to a system enables it to do work. This, by definition, means that heat is a form of energy.

When the first law was proposed, many people found it difficult to accept because they did not believe that heat was a form of energy. They thought of it as a mysterious fluid. But the first law did describe the action of heat engines and of many other kinds of heat interactions, so it came to be accepted as valid.

THE SECOND LAW

The first law says that the total energy of the universe remains constant. It does not say what kinds of energy can be changed into what other kinds of energy. After many false starts, a principle—the second law of thermodynamics—was worked out that described the kinds of energy conversions that are possible.

William Thomson, Baron Kelvin, who played a major role in the development of the second law of thermodynamics. Hulton Archive/Getty Images

This law states that conditions within any system tend to change to a condition of maximum disorder. (The amount of disorder in a system is called entropy.) Work must therefore be done from outside the system to impose more order on the system—that is, to decrease its entropy.

The second law of thermodynamics may seem surprising, yet it does describe many common experiences. For example, when someone kicks off his or her shoes, it is far more likely that they will land not in the closet where they belong but somewhere else. To get them where they belong, the person must exert work. He or she must pick them up, carry them to the closet, and place them in their proper location.

Heat energy is the most disordered form of energy. (The individual molecules in an object move in random directions.) Therefore, according to the second law, only a fraction of the heat energy available can be converted to useful work. Heat engines can transform some but not all of the heat energy available to them into mechanical energy. The rest remains as heat energy whether or not it is needed, wanted, or welcome.

PERPETUAL-MOTION MACHINES

For hundreds of years, people have tried to make perpetual-motion machines. Once set in motion, such a device would continue in motion forever, with no additional energy required to maintain it. These machines are impossible, however, according to the laws of thermodynamics. Even after these laws were discovered in the 19th century, many inventors, dreamers, and con artists have still tried to break, get around, or ignore those laws. The enormous appeal of perpetual motion resides in the promise of a virtually free and limitless source of power.

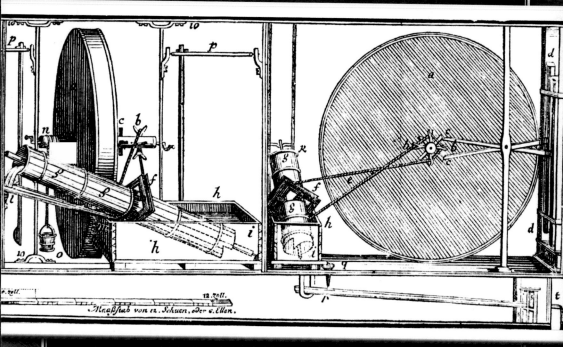

Diagram of a purported perpetual-motion machine designed by Johann Bessler (known as Orffyreus). © Photos.com/Jupiterimages

Some people have proposed perpetual-motion machines that would purportedly deliver more energy from a falling or turning body than is required to restore those devices to their original state. This type of machine would produce more energy than it consumes. It would thus violate the first law of thermodynamics, which states that the total energy of an isolated system is always constant.

A second kind of perpetual-motion machine relies on being able to convert heat energy completely to work and other forms of energy, with no heat energy left over. This is impossible, however, according to the second law of thermodynamics.

Still other types of perpetual-motion machines have been proposed based on misunderstandings of the nature of certain energy sources. An example is the self-winding clock that derives energy from changes in the temperature or pressure of the atmosphere. It depends upon the energy delivered to Earth by the Sun and is not, therefore, a perpetual-motion machine.

Mechanical energy, on the other hand, can be completely converted to heat energy. This is a significant difference. In both conversions, the total amount of energy is conserved. But the second law of thermodynamics describes a restriction in the direction in which the conversions of energy can take place.

An automobile engine changes the chemical energy of gasoline into heat energy. The heat energy causes the gas to expand and push on a piston, thereby changing the heat energy partially to mechanical energy. Much of the heat energy, however, simply heats up the engine. The mechanical energy of the pistons is transferred to the tires, which push against the road's surface and move the car forward. But some of the energy in the tires is changed to heat energy by friction. In this and in all other processes involving conversions of heat energy to mechanical energy, much of the original heat energy remains.

To illustrate the difference between the second law of thermodynamics and the first, consider a pan of water that is heated by a burner. The first law of thermodynamics would perfectly well allow the water to freeze and the flame of the burner to get hotter, just as long as the total amount of energy remained the same. The second law of thermodynamics asserts that this is impossible. The process must proceed in the direction that transfers heat from the hotter to the colder body. The general direction of all processes occurring in the observed universe is that which increases entropy.

THE THIRD LAW

The third law of thermodynamics concerns a temperature called absolute zero. Absolute zero occurs at about −273°C (−460°F). At absolute zero, all substances theoretically would possess the minimum possible amount of energy, and some substances would possess zero entropy (be completely ordered). The third law states that, while absolute zero may be approached more and more closely, it is impossible to actually reach it.

Conclusion

As we have seen, energy is the capacity to do work. All of the many forms of energy are thus associated with motion. This property is most obvious with kinetic energy, which is the energy an object or particle has because it is moving. Potential energy is the energy that an entity, such as a stretched rubber band, has because of its position. This energy gives the rubber band the potential to move. If the rubber band is released, its potential energy is changed to kinetic energy, and the rubber band flies through the air.

Chemical and nuclear energy are forms of potential energy stored in the bonds of chemical compounds and in the nuclei of atoms, respectively. Electrical energy is the energy of an electric current—the movement of charged particles. Radiant energy, such as that of light, moves in waves. Heat energy is the energy something has because of the random motion of its individual molecules.

Energy can be converted from one form to another. Heat energy, however, is more disordered than other kinds of energy. The heat energy in a system can never be completely changed to other types of energy. But regardless of the types of energy conversion, the total amount of energy in an isolated system always remains the same.

Energy and matter together form the basis of all observable phenomena in the universe, so the study of energy is fundamental to the study of the physical world. All that is known about energy also enables the creation of innovative devices that make life easier and more enjoyable. In fact, the industrialized world depends on the harnessing of energy to light, heat, and cool its homes and businesses, to power its machinery, and to fuel its transportation vehicles. As such, energy technology is sure to remain a major focus of development in the future.

absolute zero The ultimate lowest temperature, which is equal to 459.67° F (-273.15° C), which can be approached but never reached.

combustion A chemical reaction, usually involving oxygen, that produces heat and light (as in a flame).

current A stream of electric charge.

entropy The degree of disorder, or randomness, in a system.

fission The splitting of an atomic nucleus resulting in the release of large amounts of energy.

friction The force of two objects rubbing against each other, which resists the motion of either or both.

fusion The union of light atomic nuclei to form heavier nuclei resulting in the release of enormous quantities of energy.

generator A machine by which mechanical energy is changed into electrical energy.

geothermal Of, relating to, or utilizing the heat of Earth's interior.

heat energy Thermal energy, or the internal energy a body or system has because of the motion of its molecules.

hydroelectric Of or relating to the production of electricity by waterpower.

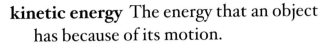

kinetic energy The energy that an object has because of its motion.

neutron An uncharged atomic particle that has a mass nearly equal to that of the proton and is present in all known atomic nuclei except the hydrogen nucleus.

nucleus The positively charged central portion of an atom that comprises nearly all of the atomic mass and that consists of protons and usually neutrons.

photon A packet of electromagnetic radiation.

photosynthesis The process by which green plants and certain other organisms transform light energy into chemical energy.

piston A sliding piece moved by or moving against the pressure of a fluid (as steam or hot gases) that usually consists of a short cylinder moving within a larger cylinder.

proton An atomic particle that occurs in the nucleus of every atom and carries a positive charge equal in size to the negative charge of an electron.

radiant energy The type of energy that travels as electromagnetic waves.

radioactivity The spontaneous giving off of rays of energy or particles by the breaking apart of atoms of certain elements (as uranium).

temperature A measure of a body's hotness or coldness, or of how fast on average its molecules are moving.

thermodynamics The branch of physics that studies relationships between heat energy, other forms of energy, and work.

thermonuclear Of, relating to, or employing transformations in the nuclei of atoms of low atomic weight (as hydrogen) that require a very high temperature for their inception (as in the hydrogen bomb or in the Sun).

turbine An engine whose central driving shaft is fitted with a series of blades spun around by the pressure of a fluid (as water, steam, or air).

work In physics, the measure of energy transfer that occurs when an object is moved over a distance by an external force, at least part of which is applied in the direction of the displacement.

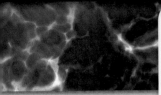

American Institute of Physics (AIP)
One Physics Ellipse
College Park, MD 20740-3843
(301) 209-3100
Web site: http://www.aip.org
The AIP seeks to promote the study of
    physics and astronomy through publica-
    tions and outreach services.

American Museum of Science and
    Energy (AMSE)
300 South Tulane Avenue
Oak Ridge, TN 37830
(865) 576-3200
Web site: http://www.amse.org
Originally founded to educate the public on
    the various uses of nuclear energy, the
    AMSE has since expanded to include
    extensive exhibits on all types of energy.

Canada Science and Technology Museum
1867 St. Laurent Boulevard
Ottawa, ON K1G 5A3
Canada
(613) 991-3044
Web site: http://www.sciencetech.
    technomuses.ca

With exhibits covering a wide array of subject areas, the Canada Science and Technology Museum inspires public interest in topics such as energy and nuclear power.

Canadian Association of Physicists (CAP)
Suite 112, MacDonald Building
University of Ottawa
150 Louis Pasteur Private
Ottawa, ON K1N 6N5
Canada
(613) 562-5614
Web site: http://www.cap.ca
Committed to advancing research and education in the field of physics, the CAP supports a number of programs and provides resources for professionals pursuing physics-related careers, students, and the public at large.

National Science Foundation (NSF)
4201 Wilson Boulevard
Arlington, VA 22230
(703) 292-5111
Web site: http://www.nsf.gov
The NSF supports scientific research and advancement throughout the United

States in a variety of subject areas, including physics and physics-related fields.

U.S. Energy Information Administration (EIA)
1000 Independence Avenue SW
Washington, DC 20585
(202) 586-8800
Web site: http://www.eia.doe.gov
The EIA conducts and distributes research on energy sources and uses to facilitate understanding of its role with respect to the government, economics, and the public at large.

Web Sites

Due to the changing nature of Internet links, Rosen Educational Services has developed an online list of Web sites related to the subject of this book. This site is updated regularly. Please use this link to access the list:

http://www.rosenlinks.com/inphy/ener

Bibliography

Challoner, Jack. *Energy* (Dorling Kindersley, 2000).

Farndon, John. *Energy* (Benchmark, 2003).

Fleisher, Paul. *Matter and Energy* (Lerner, 2009).

Garrett, Leslie. *Dictionary of Forces, Matter, and Energy* (Celebration Press, 2005).

Kahan, Peter. *Motion, Forces, and Energy* (Prentice Hall, 2002).

Nardo, Don. *Kinetic Energy: The Energy of Motion* (Compass Point, 2008).

Parker, Steve, and Pang, Alex, illus. *Energy and Power* (Mason Crest, 2011).

Smith, Alastair. *Energy, Forces, and Motion* (EDC, 2002).

Snedden, Robert. *Energy Transfer,* rev. ed. (Heinemann, 2007).

Solway, Andrew, ed. *Energy and Matter* (Brown Bear, 2010).

Tabak, John. *Nuclear Energy* (Facts on File, 2009).

Whyman, Kathryn. *Energy and Heat* (Stargazer, 2005).

Index